PIANO MUSIC OF
AMY BEACH

Compiled and Edited by Gail Smith

ISBN 978-1-4803-5286-5

7777 W. BLUEMOUND RD. P.O. BOX 13819 MILWAUKEE, WI 53213

Visit Hal Leonard Online at
www.halleonard.com

Contents

4 Amy Beach Biography

6 About the Music

9 Scottish Legend, Op. 54, No. 1

12 A Hermit Thrush at Morn, Op. 92, No. 2

19 Fire-Flies
from *Four Sketches*, Op. 15, No. 4

28 In Autumn
from *Four Sketches*, Op. 15, No. 1

34 Bal masque, Op. 22

40 Arctic Night
from *Eskimos: Four Characteristic Pieces*, Op. 64, No. 1

42 Menuet Italien
from *Trois morceaux caractéristiques*, Op. 28, No. 2

49 From Blackbird Hills, Op. 83

56 Honeysuckle
from *From Grandmother's Garden*, Op. 97, No. 5

62 Variations on Balkan Themes, Op. 60

86 Important Dates in the Life of Amy Beach

Amy Marcy Cheney Beach

(1867–1944)

Amy Marcy Cheney was born on September 5, 1867 in Henniker, New Hampshire. Amy's mother was Clara Imogene Marcy, a talented singer and pianist. Her father, Charles Abbott, entered college at age 16, graduated from Bates College and became a paper manufacturer and importer.

Amy could sing 40 tunes when she was only one year old. Before the age of two, she could harmonize an alto line with her mother. Her parents soon realized that their child was gifted. It was discovered Amy associated colors with certain tonal areas; she would ask her mother to play the "pink music." A piece in E-flat Major was pink to her; the color violet was the key of D-flat Major. Amy was reading by age three and memorizing lengthy poems. At age four she composed three waltzes in her head while visiting her grandparents. Upon arriving home, she amazed her mother by playing them. Soon Amy began lessons with her mother and when just seven years old played a Beethoven sonata and other pieces in recital.

The family moved to Boston and Amy began formal piano lessons with Mr. Ernst Perabo. At the age of ten, she went along with her mother to visit relatives in California. There, a friend of the family found out that Amy had perfect pitch and took her out in the country to help notate bird calls. During one day they notated twenty different bird calls. The notations of the many California larks became Amy's contribution to ornithological science. The notations were included along with an article in a scientific journal.

When Amy was 16 she made her debut with the Boston Symphony Orchestra performing Mosceles' Concerto in G minor at the Boston Music Hall. The same year, Amy's first published composition was the vocal solo "The Rainy Day," with words by Henry Wadsworth Longfellow, composed four years earlier. Amy's next piano teacher was Karl Barmann, a pupil of Franz Liszt. Amy also took harmony with Junius W. Hill, an organist, composer, and later a professor at Wellesley College.

On December 2, 1885 she married the famous Boston surgeon and Harvard Medical School graduate, Dr. Henry Harris Aubrey Beach, and thereafter was called Mrs. H.H.A. Beach. Her husband, more than twice her age, played piano, sang, and wrote poems. Amy Beach spent most of her time composing music during 25 years of marriage. She gave a few recitals for charity but her husband forbade her to teach piano. She studied many treatises on music, sometimes translating them from French and German, and had copies of most everything ever written on composition, theory, and orchestration available at the time. Beach studied on her own and was extremely disciplined. Soon after marriage, she began composing the "Mass in E-flat," premiered by the Handel & Haydn Society in Boston, the first composition by a woman performed there.

Dr. Beach died in 1910 when Amy was 42 years old. The widow sailed to Europe and remained there for four years, performing her piano concerto with many orchestras. For the rest of her life, Beach divided her time between composing and performing. She spent most summers at the MacDowell Colony composing, and concertizing all over the United States during the rest of the year. Beach was commissioned to compose many works for special occasions. She said, "the process of musical composition cannot be reduced to any single formula, because each type of music sets its own creative pattern." She also stated (using the masculine pronoun common in her period), "the composer must have emotional and spiritual feeling to put into his work; he must achieve a comprehensible translation of his feeling through form; and he must have at his disposal a tremendous background of technical, musical craftsmanship in order to express his feelings and his thoughts. Thus, the craftsmanship, vital though it is, serves chiefly as the means toward the end of personal expression."

Amy Beach died on December 27, 1944 in New York City of a heart ailment. She was 77 years old. She was praised in her day by Presidents and Kings. Her music is classic and in the 21st century we are re-discovering the vast spectrum of her creations. Recently her name was added to the famous "Hatch Shell" in Boston. Beach is now the only woman carved in granite with over seventy other composers such as Chopin, Bach and Beethoven. She was the first woman in America known to have composed a symphony. She composed hundreds of other compositions that include a piano concerto, an opera, numerous piano solos and duets, a violin sonata, chamber music, many choral anthems, and vocal solos.

About the Music

Scottish Legend, Op. 54, No. 1

This lovely piece was first published in 1903 by Arthur P. Schmidt Company. Beach captured the essence of a Scottish folk melody in her original composition. The first sixteen measures express a feeling of rich harmonic texture in D minor. The animated middle section is in the parallel major, returning to D minor again to bring the lyrical legend to perfect closure.

A Hermit Thrush at Morn, Op. 92, No. 2

This enchanting piece was inspired by a hermit thrush singing perched in a tree outside Beach's studio at the MacDowell Colony. It was during the summer of 1921, the first time that she had come to this 400-acre haven to compose at the invitation of Marian MacDowell, the widow of Edward MacDowell. The actual bird call can be heard throughout this peaceful piano solo.

Fire-Flies from *Four Sketches*, Op. 15, No. 4

This miniature tone poem was first published in 1892 by Arthur P. Schmidt Company. It is a dazzling show piece with shimmering descending thirds. The famous concert pianist Josef Hofmann often played this work in recitals.

In Autumn from *Four Sketches*, Op. 15, No. 1

"Feuillages jaunissants sur les gazons epars." ("Yellowing foliage scattered on the grass.") This line of French poetry by Alphonse de Lamartine appeared at the top of the music. Beach celebrates the fall season while painting a musical picture of colored leaves dancing in the wind.

Bal masque, Op. 22

This waltz was published in 1894 by Arthur Schmidt Company. As a child, one of the first pieces Amy learned was a Strauss waltz she heard her mother playing at the piano. Waltzes were among the first pieces she composed at the age of four. "Bal masque" (masked ball) has all the excitement of a Grande Ball in Vienna, opening with a long trill and introduction, giving the dancers time to get out on the dance floor. The piece begins in G Major, the key Beach identified with the color red, and modulates to E-flat Major music with the melody in the bass. A spectacular modulation occurs at the "golden mean" bringing the music back to the key of G, dancing all the way to the end.

Arctic Night from *Eskimos: Four Characteristic Pieces*, Op. 64, No. 1

This piece was published in 1907 by Arthur Schmidt Company. It is the first movement in the Eskimos Suite. This slow expressive piece in C minor is based on an Inuit Native American folk song. Beach played this suite at a recital on July 28, 1917 in Concord, New Hampshire after a brief lecture on Eskimo music.

Menuet Italien from *Trois morceaux caractéristiques*, Op. 28, No. 2

This charming menuet was first composed in 1877 when Amy was only ten years old. Years later she composed a different version, making it more difficult by thickening the textures with rich layered harmonies adding a lovely middle section in C minor. The music modulates back to the menuet with a quasi cadenza.

From Blackbird Hills, Op. 83

This dramatic piece, published in 1922, is based on an Omaha Tribal Dance. The melody is a ring dance, sung and danced by children in the tribe. The bass sound suggests the drum beat and stomping feet. Beach explained that in the *Adagio molto* section she pictured members of the tribe "looking sadly over the shoulders of the happy living children at play."

Honeysuckle from *From Grandmother's Garden*, Op. 97, No. 5

This suite was published in 1922. Beach was inspired by nature and loved flowers. "Honeysuckle" is the final piece in the suite and depicts a twisting vine with sweet smelling flowers. The harmony is contemporary and at times dissonant.

Variations on Balkan Themes, Op. 60

This is considered Amy Beach's longest and most difficult piano solo. It is a concert piece based on Balkan folk songs. Reverend William Washburn Sleeper was a professor at Wellesley College and a Protestant missionary to Bulgaria. He lectured on Balkan music and customs. While in Bulgaria, he collected many folk songs, which he shared with Beach. An uprising of Macedonian nationalists in 1904 provoked cruel treatment by the Turks and general political unrest in the area. In an effort to raise awareness of human rights violations, Beach assembled an audience to hear about the political developments abroad in the spring of 1904. She asked Reverend Sleeper for copies of the folk songs, but the copies did not arrive quickly enough. Beach remembered the Balkan melodies and composed the opus 60 variations before receiving music. She told someone she had transcribed from memory only one note incorrectly. Beach used four of the Balkan folk songs in her composition. The main theme is the Serbian song "O Maiko moya," appearing in each of the eight variations. The composer premiered the work on February 8, 1905, at a recital at Huntington Chambers Hall in Boston at a benefit for the Faelten Piano School.

Scottish Legend
Op. 54, No. 1

Amy Marcy Beach
(1867–1944)

Lento con molto espressione (♩ = c. 63)

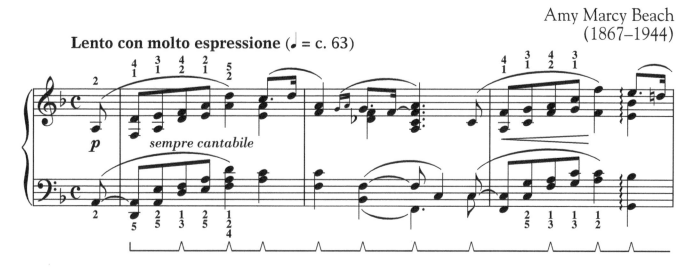

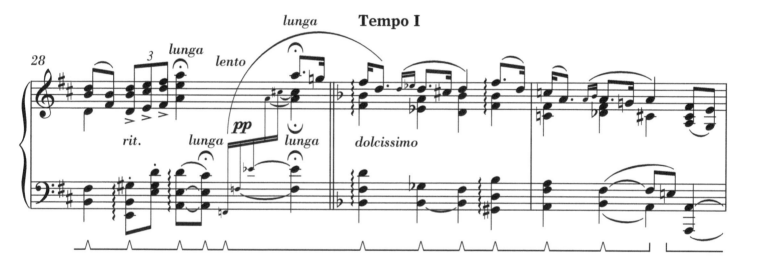

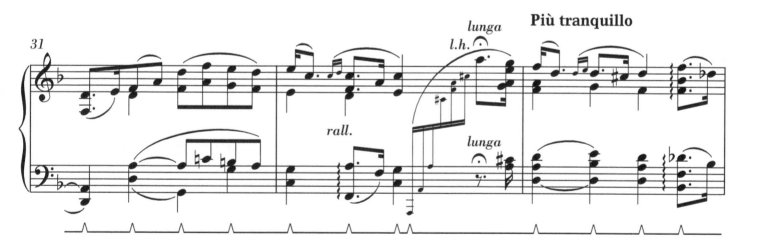

A Hermit Thrush at Morn
Op. 92, No. 2

Amy Marcy Beach
(1867–1944)

*These bird-calls are exact notations of hermit thrush songs, in the original keys but an octave lower, obtained at Mac Dowell Colony, Peterborough, N.H.

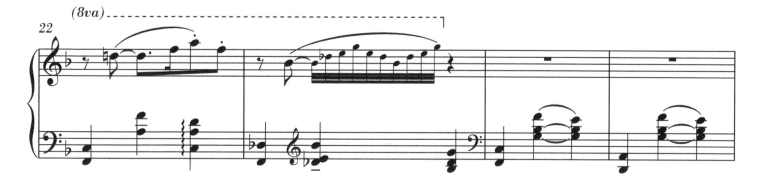

Poco agitato

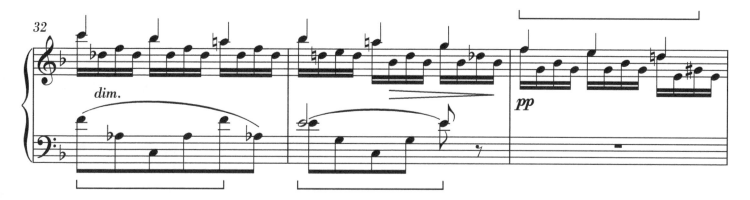

melodia marcata

espressivo

Tempo I

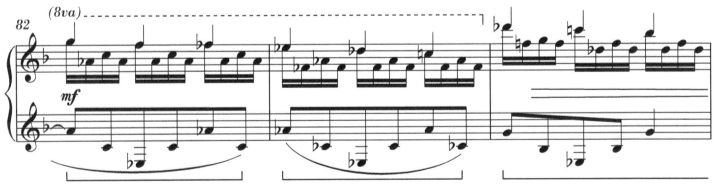

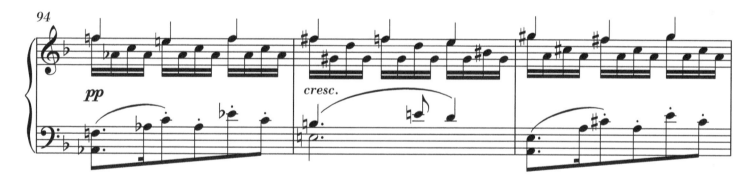

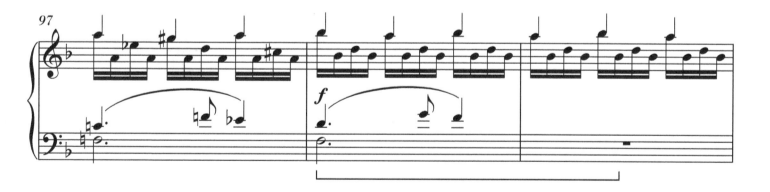

18

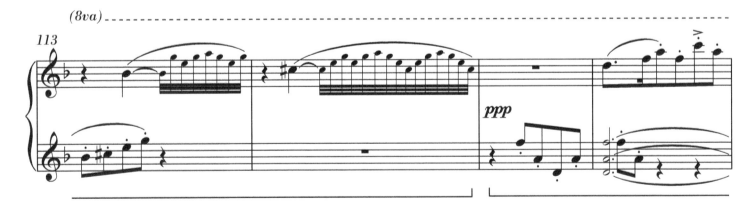

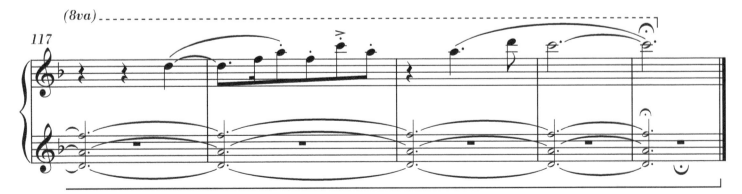

Fire-Flies

from *Four Sketches*, Op. 15, No. 4

Amy Marcy Beach
(1867–1944)

Allegro vivace

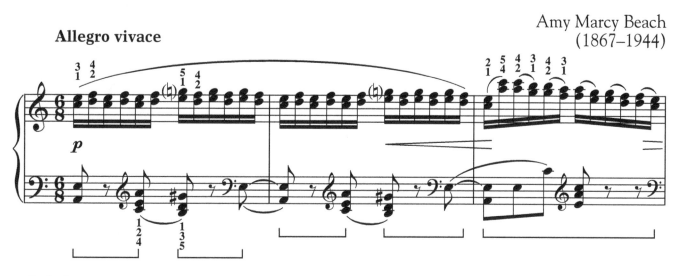

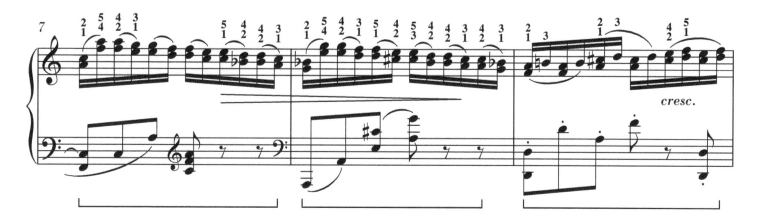

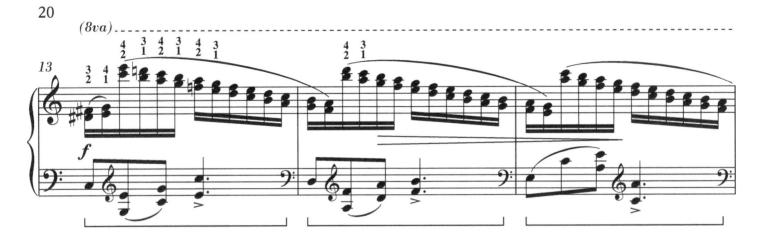

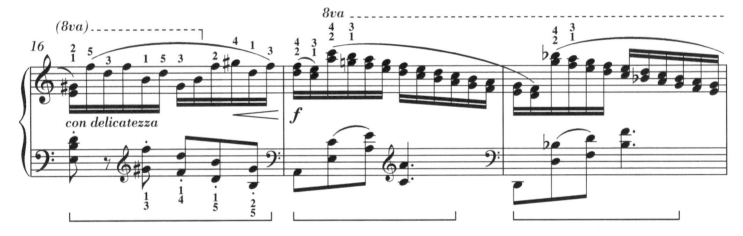

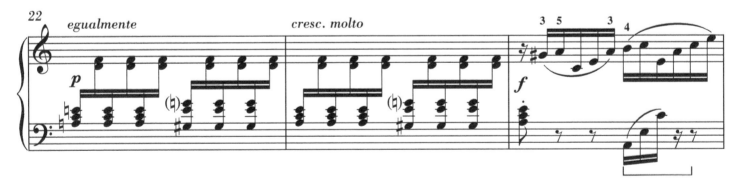

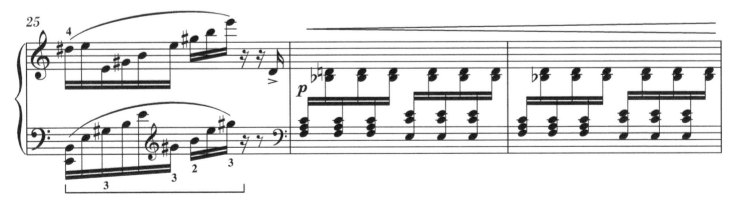

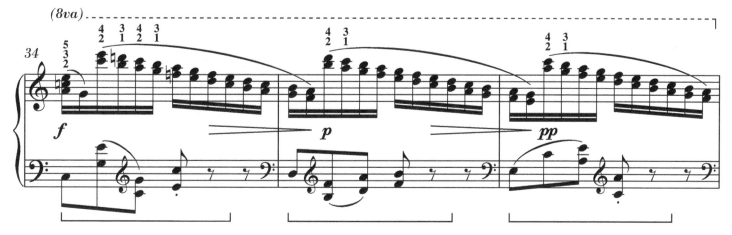

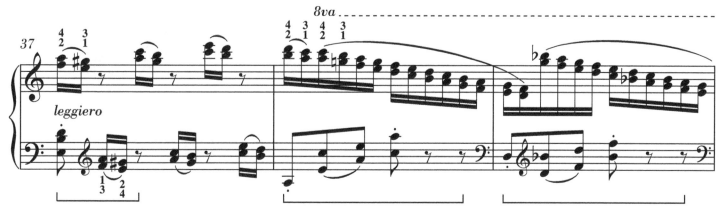

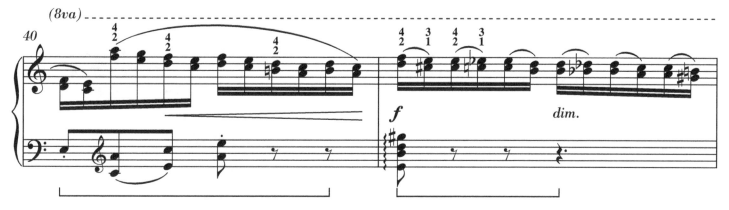

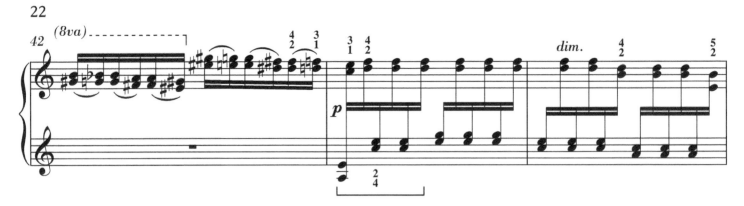

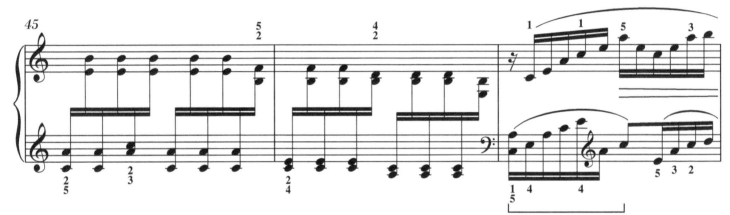

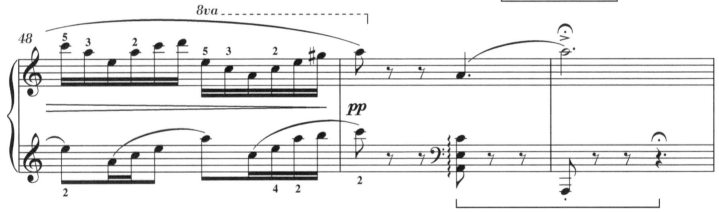

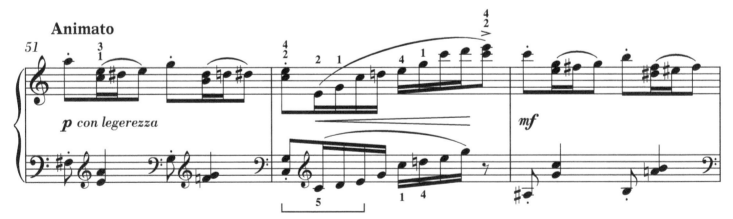

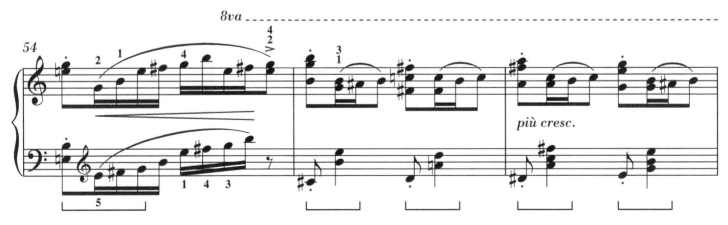

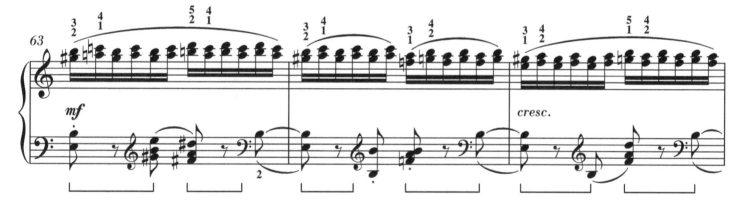

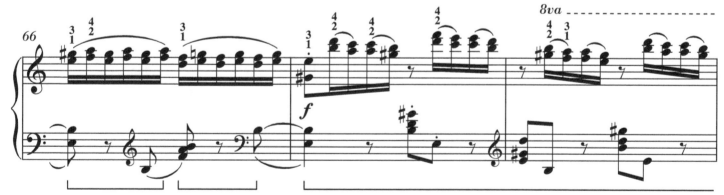

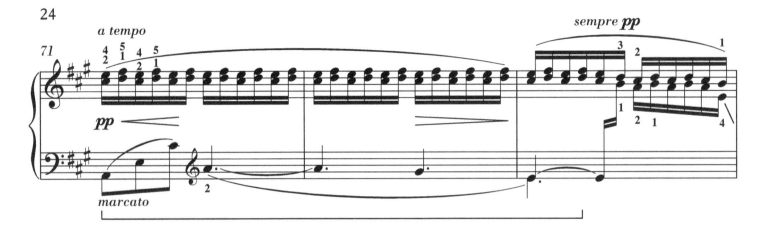

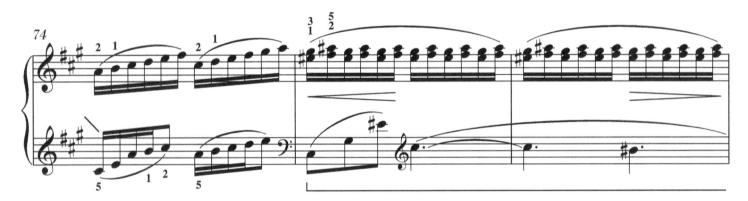

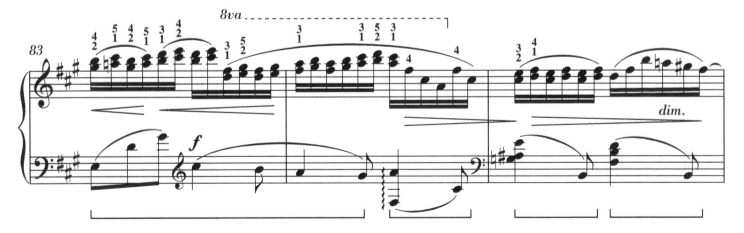

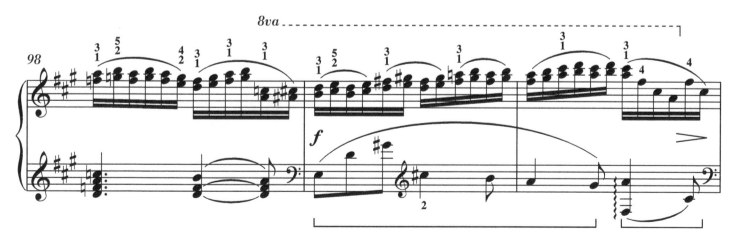

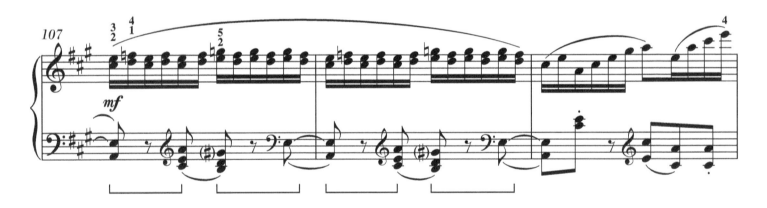

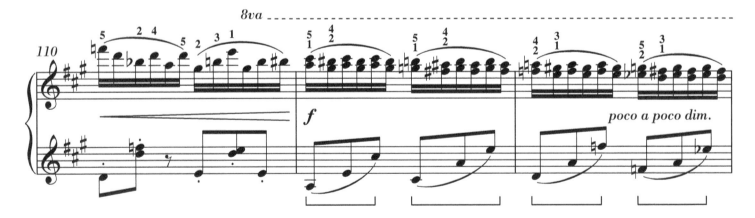

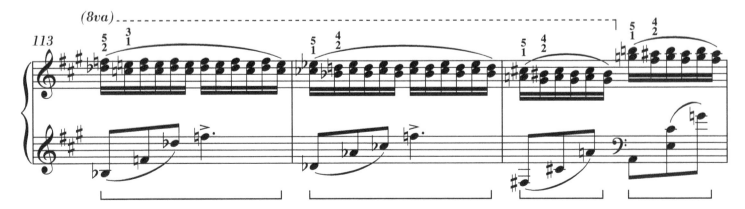

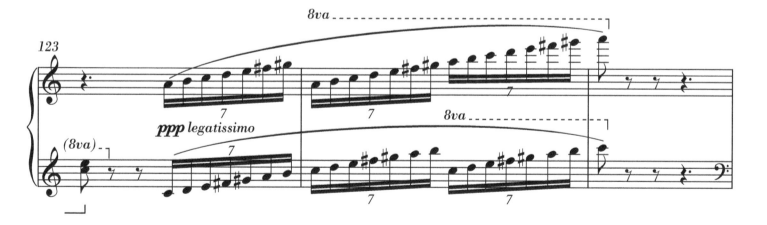

In Autumn

from *Four Sketches*, Op. 15, No. 1

Amy Marcy Beach
(1867–1944)

Allegro ma non tanto

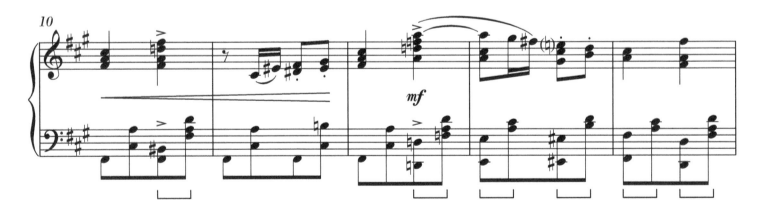

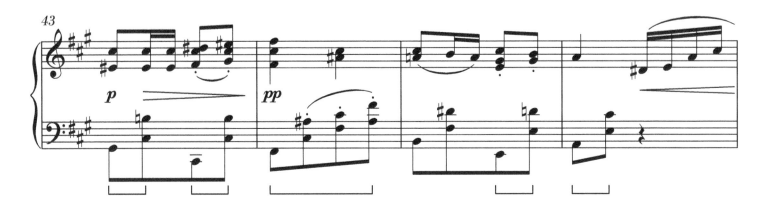

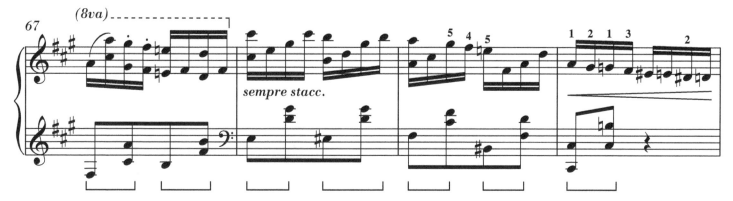

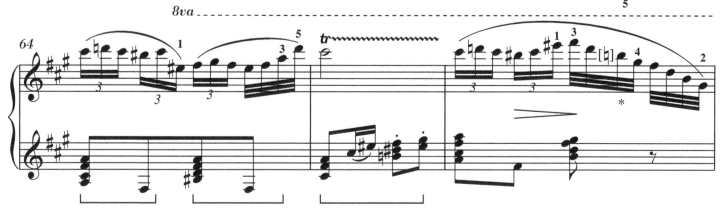

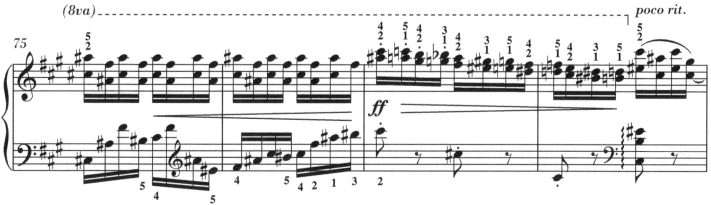

*B-sharp in the first edition.

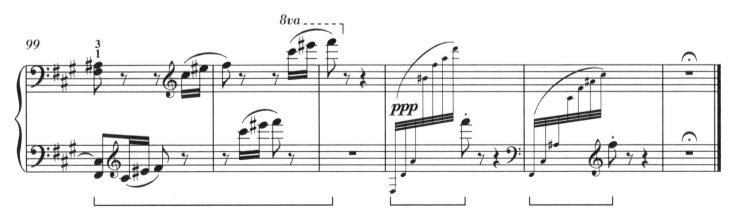

This page has been left blank
to facilitate page turns

Bal masqué
Op. 22

Amy Marcy Beach
(1867–1944)

Tempo di Valse

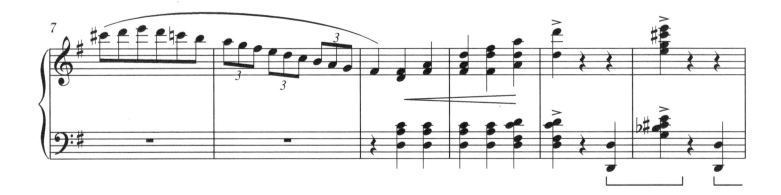

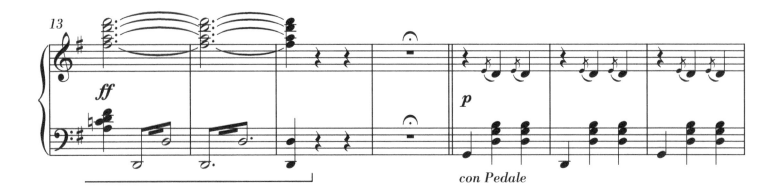

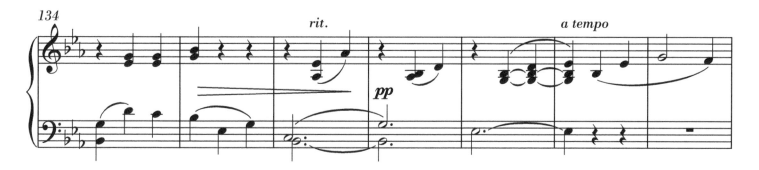

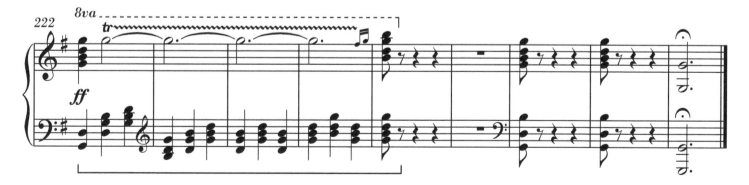

Arctic Night

from *Eskimos: Four Characteristic Pieces*, Op. 64, No. 1

Amy Marcy Beach
(1867–1944)

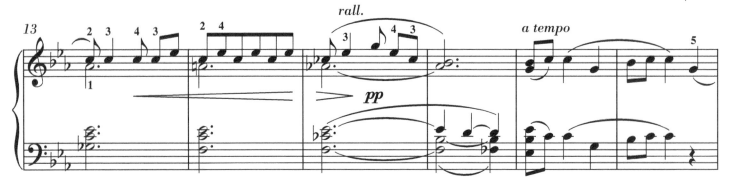

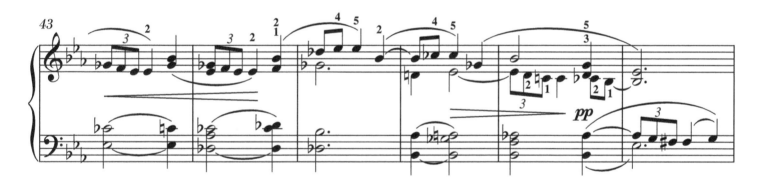

Menuet Italien

from *Trois morceaux caractéristiques*, Op. 28, No. 2

Amy Marcy Beach
(1867–1944)

Allegretto con delicatezza

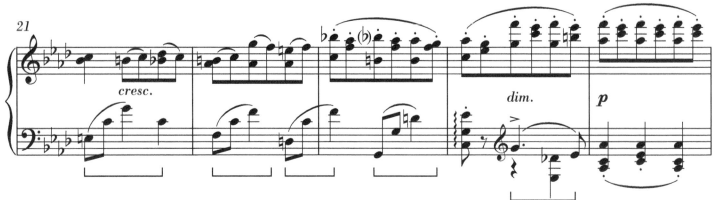

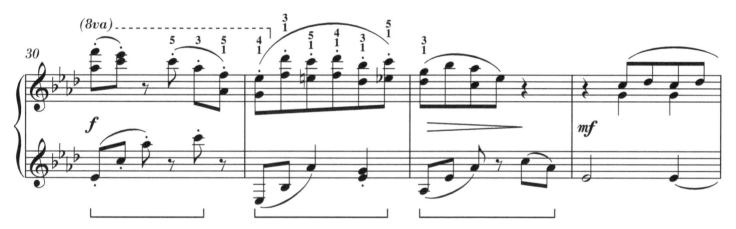

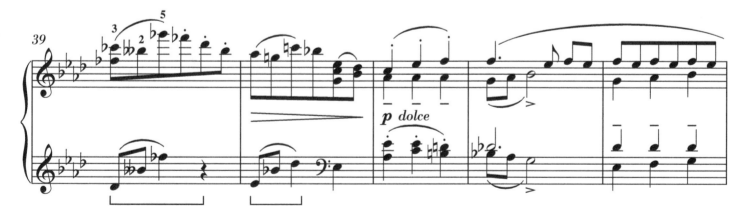

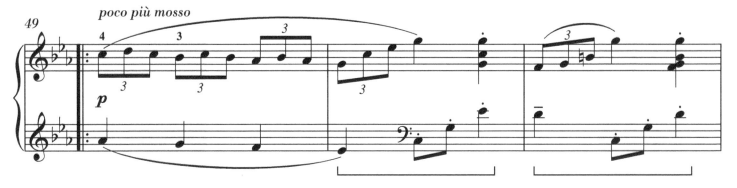

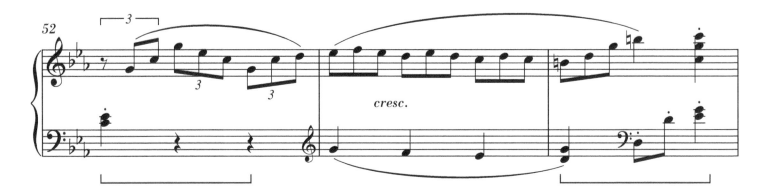

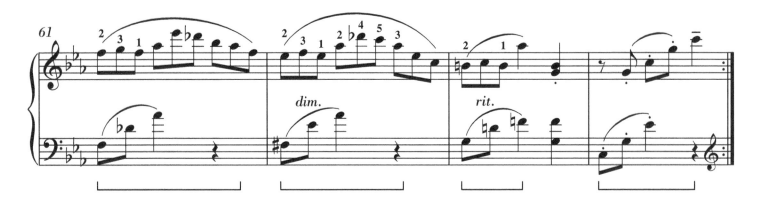

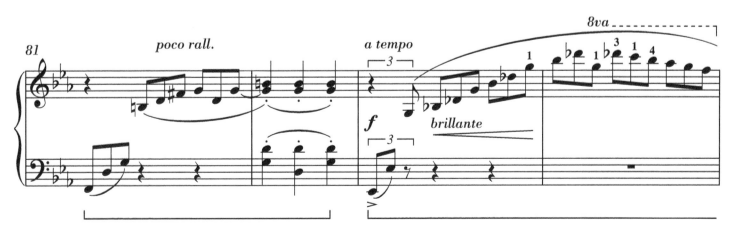

Tempo I

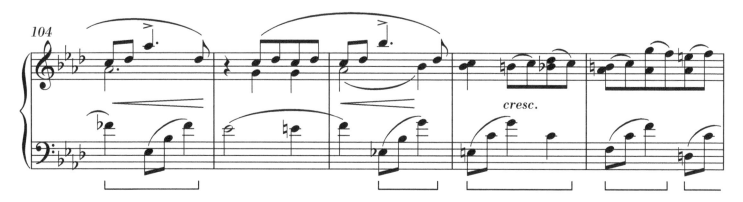

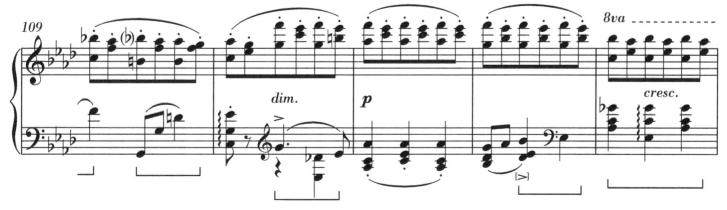

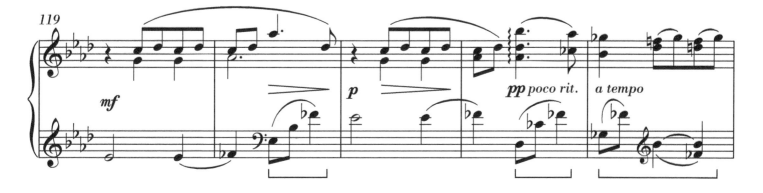

This page has been left blank
to facilitate page turns

To Miss Gertrude Kinscella

From Blackbird Hills
(An Omaha Tribal Dance)
Op. 83

Amy Marcy Beach
(1867–1944)

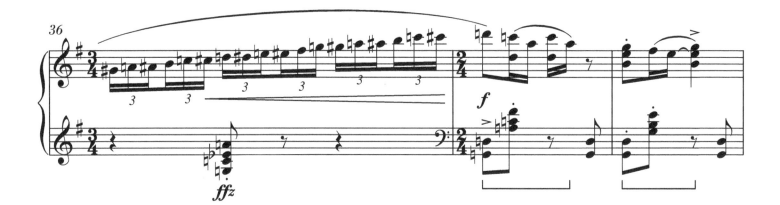

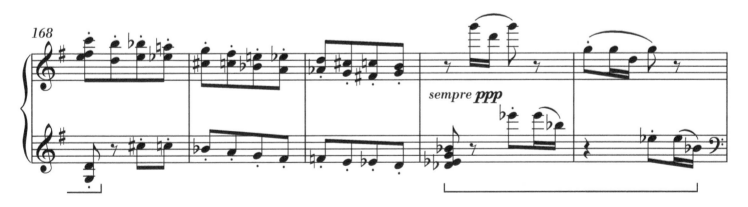

Honeysuckle

from *From Grandmother's Garden*, Op. 97, No. 5

Amy Marcy Beach
(1867–1944)

Allegro di Molto, con delicatezza

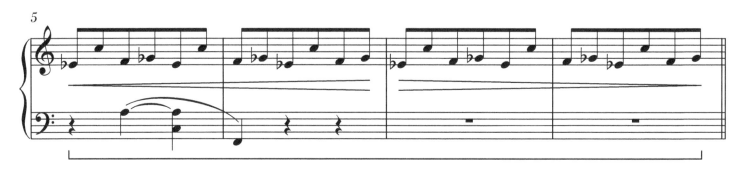

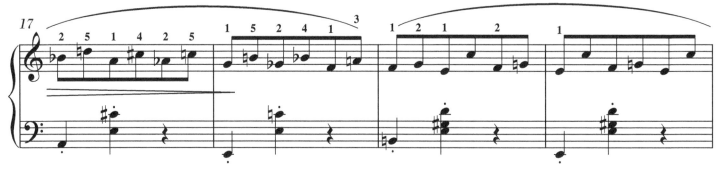

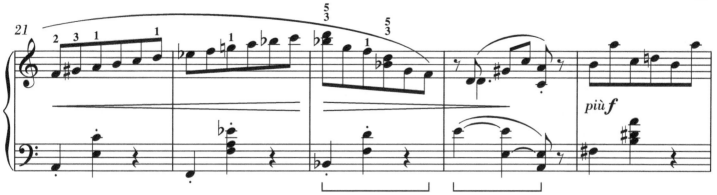

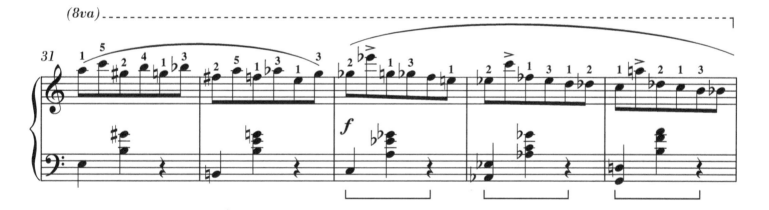

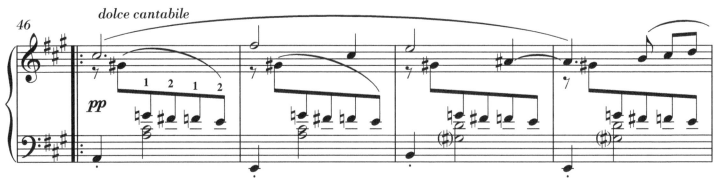

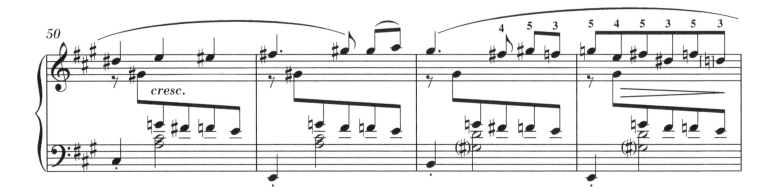

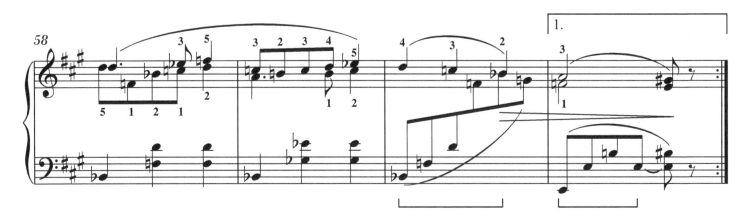

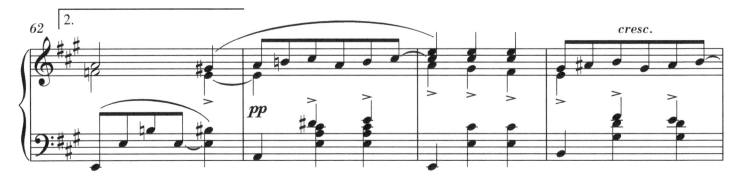

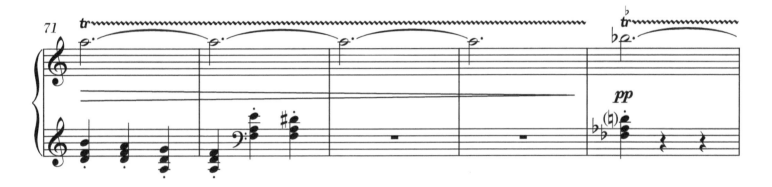

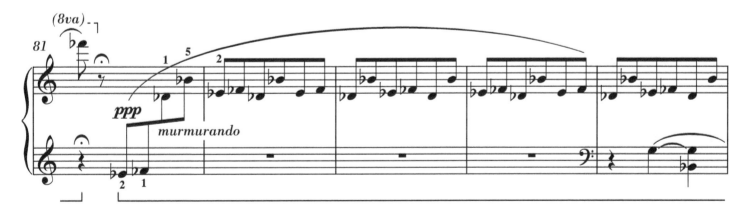

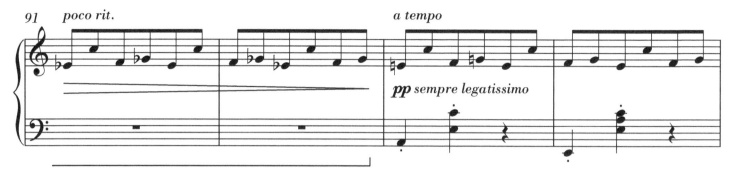

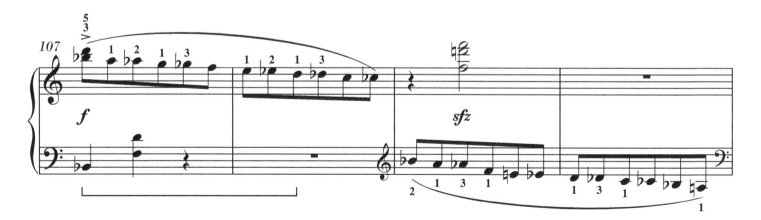

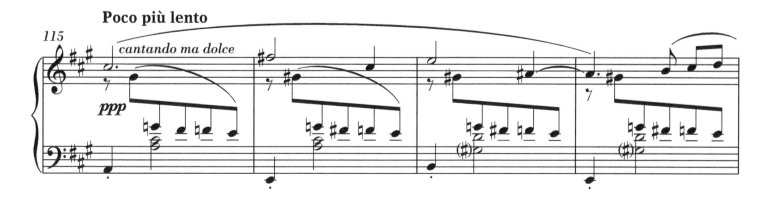

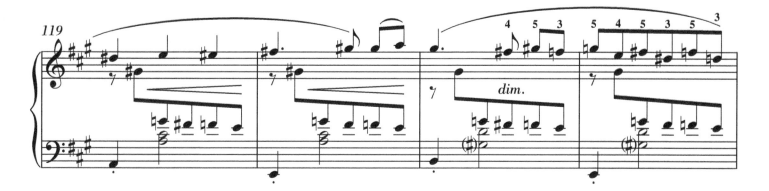

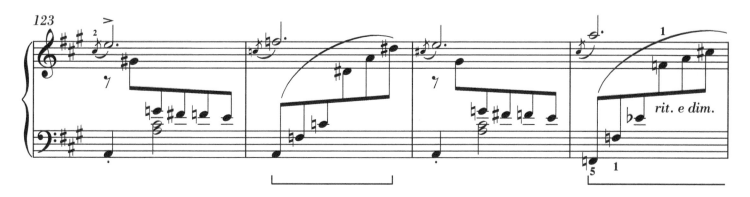

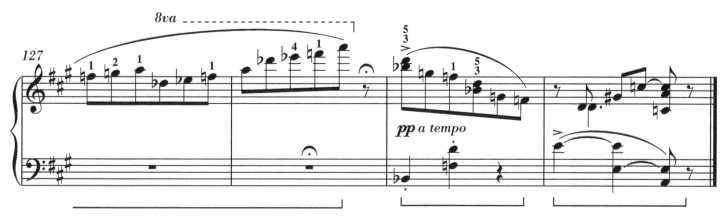

Variations on Balkan Themes
Op. 60

Amy Marcy Beach
(1867–1944)

Adagio malincolico (♩ = 66)

sempre cantando

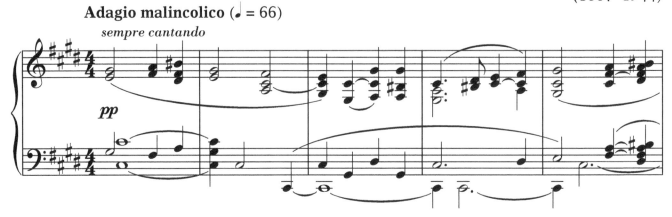

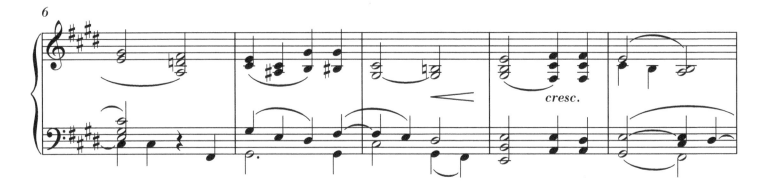

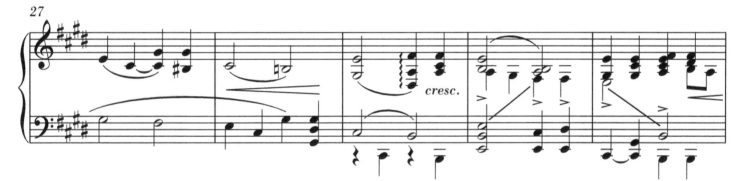

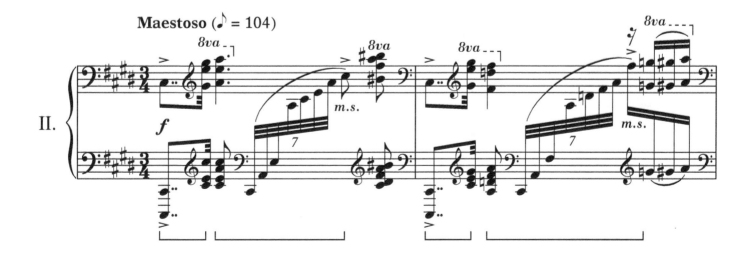

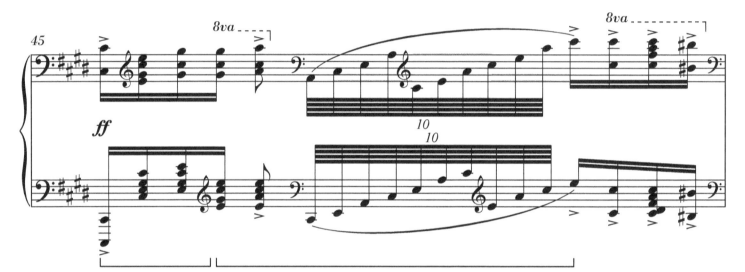

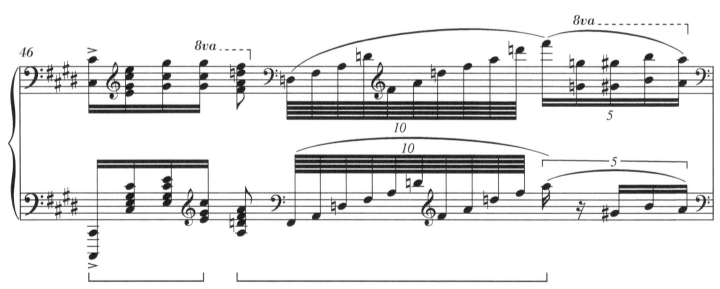

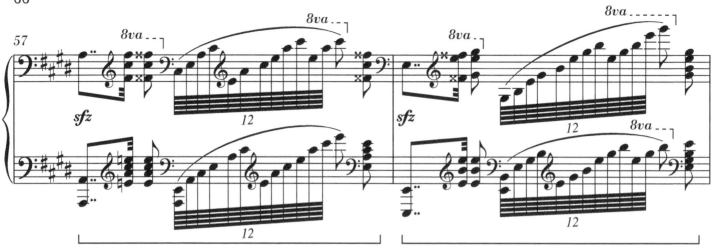

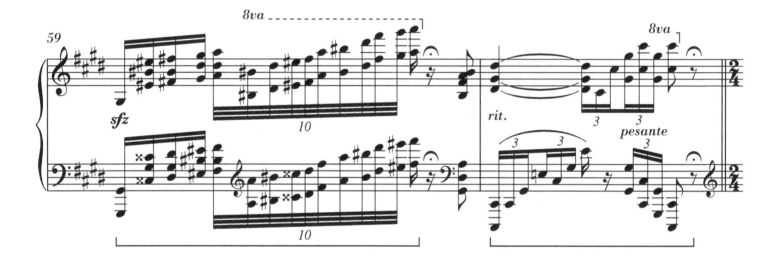

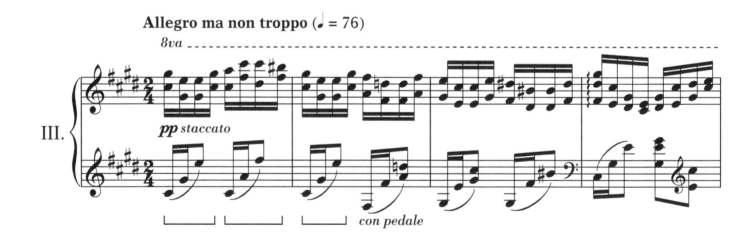

Allegro ma non troppo (♩ = 76)

III.

pp staccato

con pedale

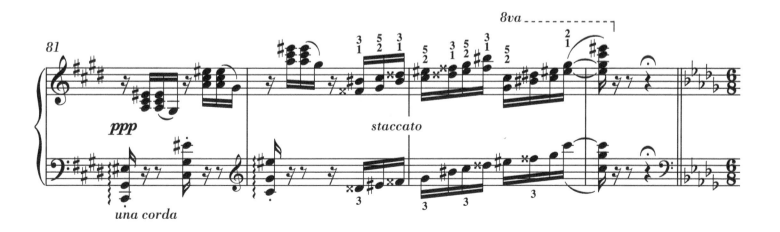

Andante alla Barcarola (♩. = 100)

IV.

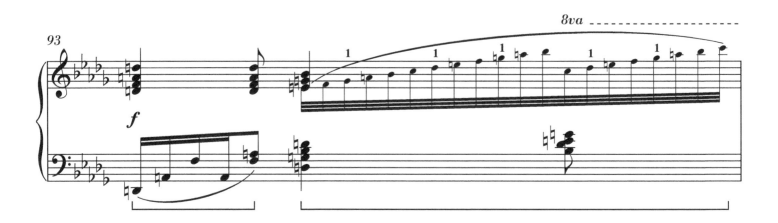

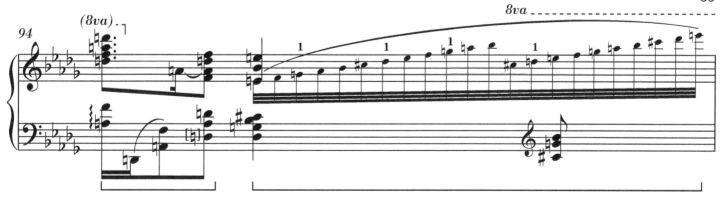

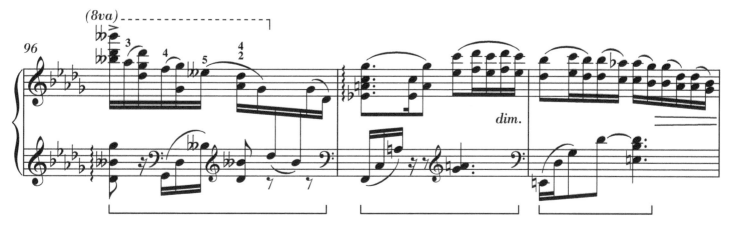

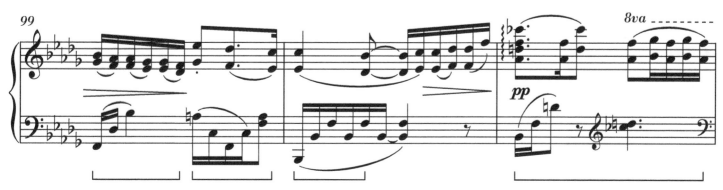

Largo con molta espressione ($\bullet$ = 42)

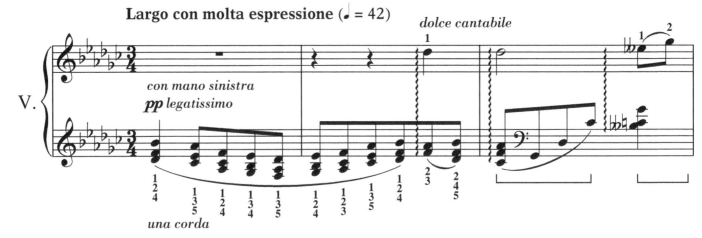

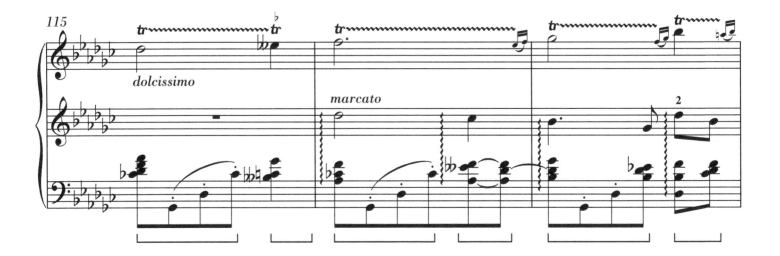

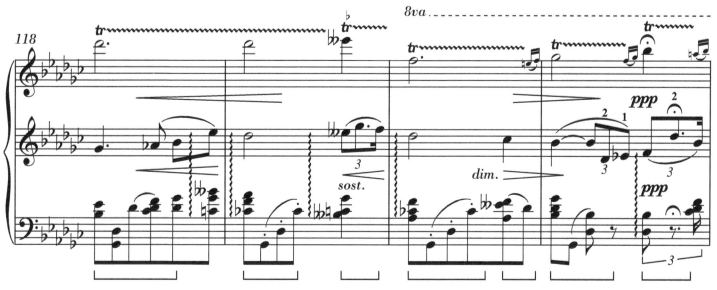

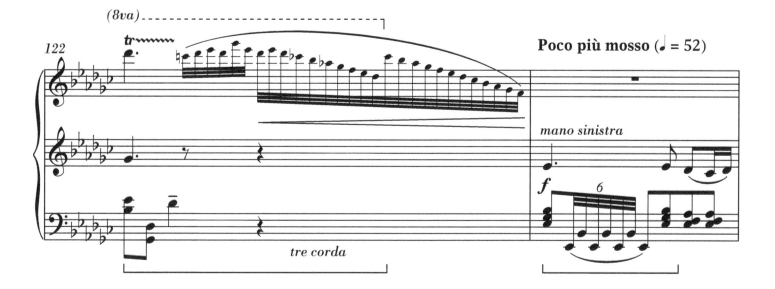

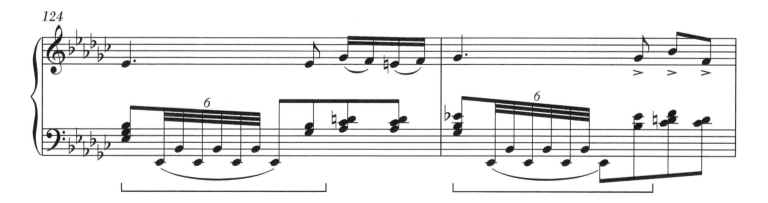

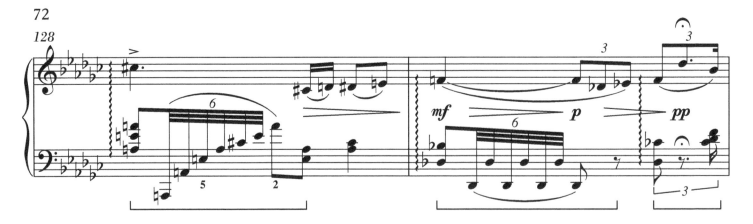

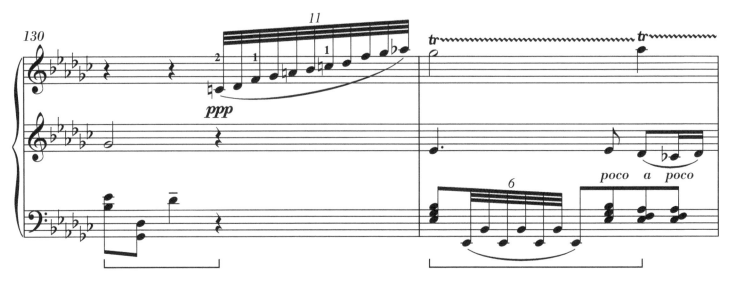

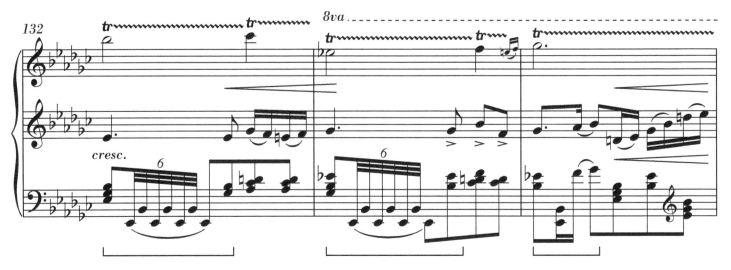

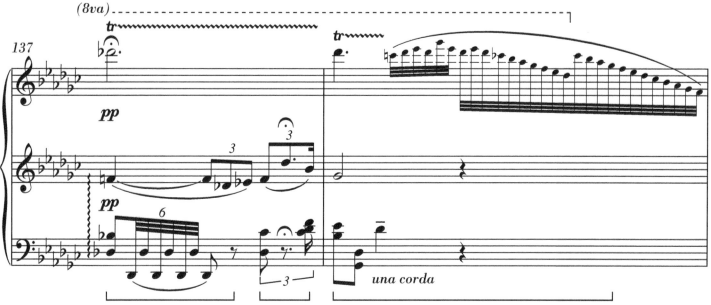

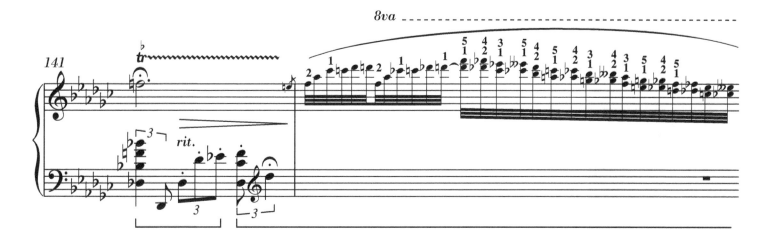

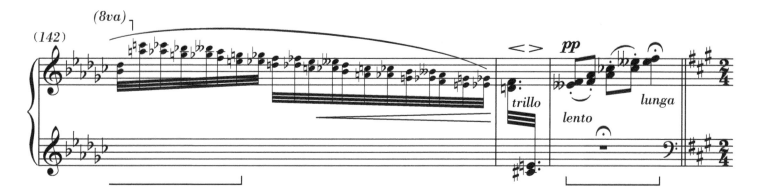

Quasi Fantasia (♩ = 60)

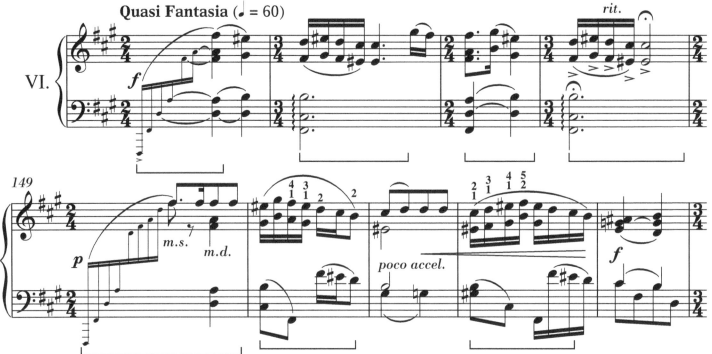

Allegro all 'Ongarese (♩ = 108)

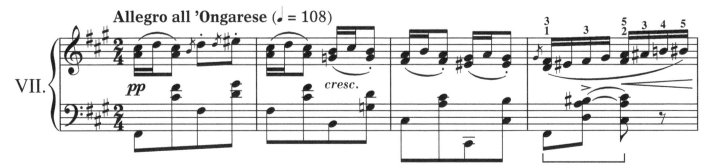

VIII.

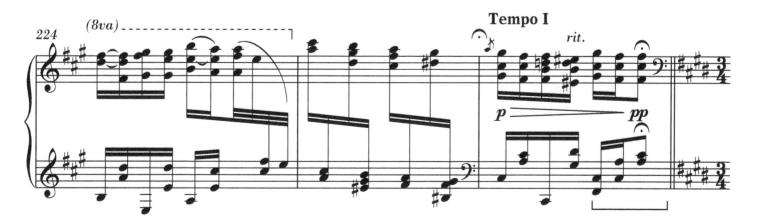

Vivace

IX.

Valse lento (*poco rubato*) (♩ = 100)

230

dolce

234

238

8va

mp

con pedale

242

poco rit.

dim.

pp

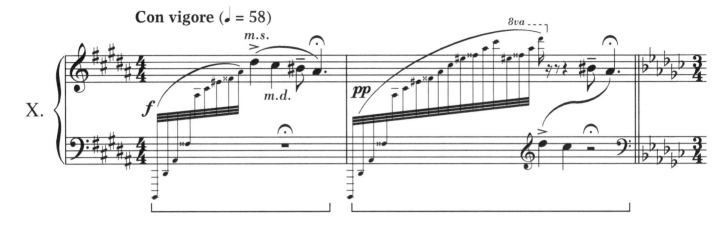

Marcia funerale (♩ = 60)

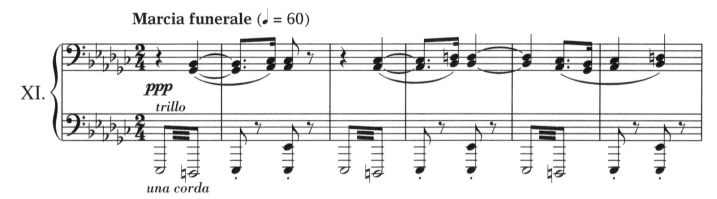

XI.

ppp

trillo

una corda

292

298

marcato
sempre **pp**

304

310

poco cresc.

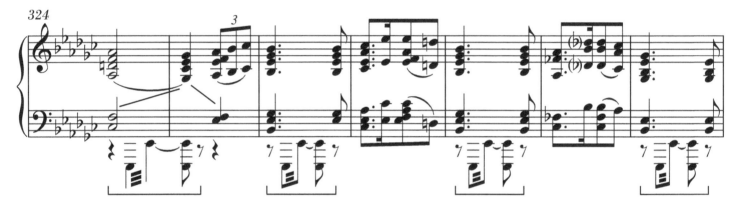

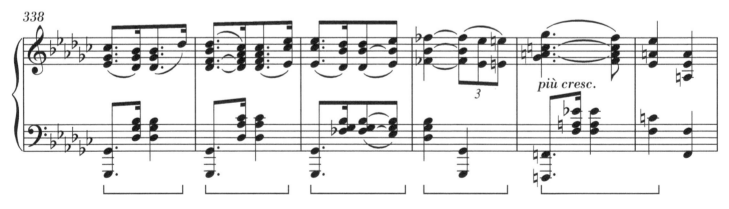

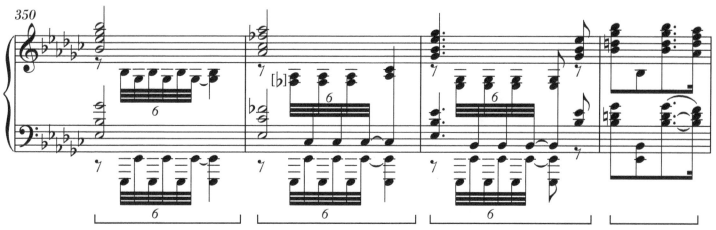

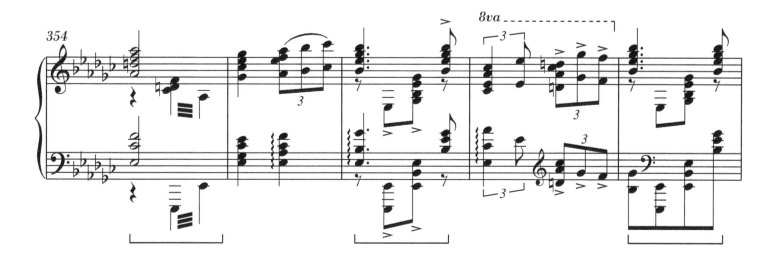

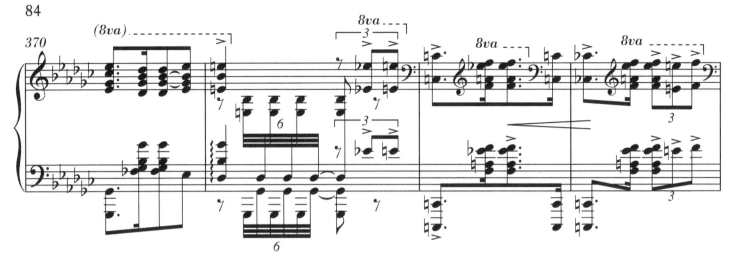

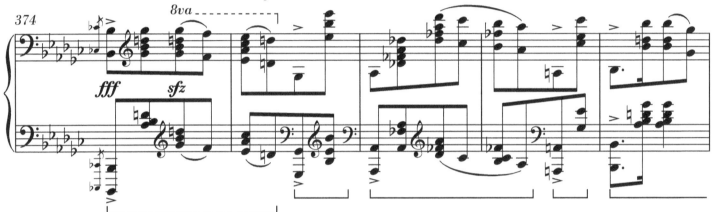

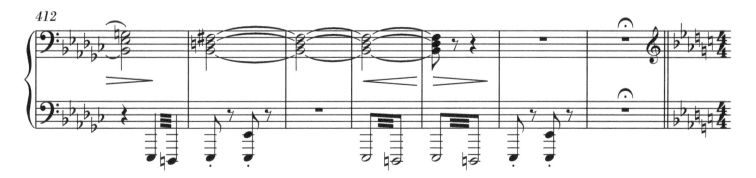

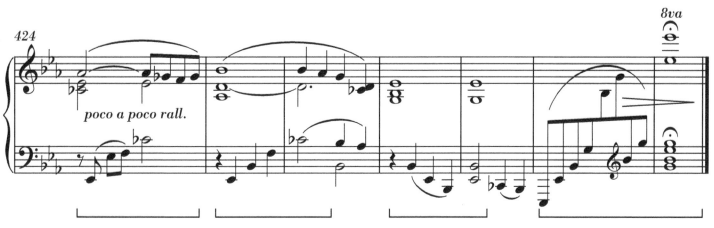

Important Dates
in the Life of Amy Beach

1867	Born September 5 in Henniker, New Hampshire
1876	Began six years of piano lessons with Johann Ernst Perabo, a German pianist who taught privately and at the New England Conservatory
1881	Began studying harmony with Junius Welch Hill at a private school
1882	Began piano lessons with Carl Baermann, a student of Franz Liszt
1883	"The Rainy Day" becomes first published composition (Oliver Ditson Company)
1883	Makes piano debut October 24 at the Music Hall in Boston performing a piece by Chopin and a concerto by Ignaz Moscheles
1885	Performed Chopin's Concerto in F minor with the Boston Symphony, March 28
1885	Beginning of a thirty-year exclusive publishing arrangement with Arthur P. Schimdt following the publication of "With Violets," Op. 1, No. 1
1885	Marries Dr. H. H. A. Beach at Trinity Church in Boston, December 2
1890	First major work, *Mass* in E-flat Major, Op. 5 was published, premiered on February 7, 1892 by the Handel and Haydn Society (This was the first time the group performed a work by a woman composer)
1893	Receives a commission to compose a piece for the dedication ceremonies of the Women's Building at The World's Columbian Exposition in Chicago
1893	Premiered *Romance*, Op. 23 for violin and piano with America's first violin virtuoso Maud Powell, July 6
1895	Charles Cheney (Amy's father) dies, July 26
1896	The Boston Symphony premieres her "Gaelic" Symphony, conducted by Emil Paur, to whom the work is dedicated, October 31
1900	Premiere of Piano Concerto in C-sharp minor by the Boston Symphony, April 7
1904	Completion of "Balkan Variations," Op. 60
1910	Dr. H.H.A. Beach dies, June 28

1911	Clara Imogene Cheney (Amy's mother) dies, February 28
1911	Sets sail for Europe
1914	Due to escalation of World War I, returns to Boston in early September
1921	Spent her first summer at the MacDowell Colony
1939	Premiere of Five Improvisations, Op. 148, and the Piano Trio, Op. 150, sponsored by the National Association of Composers and Conductors, January 15
1939	Sculptor Bashka Paeff unveils a large plaster bust of Amy Beach in her Carnegie Hall studio at a celebration attended by friends and colleagues, March 16
1940	Final recital in Brooklyn, March 19
1944	Dies December 29 from complications of the heart condition. Funeral services are held at St. Bartholomew's in New York City. Later an urn with her ashes is taken to Boston where it is interred in the Forest Hills Cemetery next to the graves of her husband and family.